Malcolm Shuttleworth

Englische Schimpfwörter von A bis Z

Aus dem Englischen
von Christopher Heil und Julia Smith

Anaconda

Die Deutsche Nationalbibliothek verzeichnet diese Publikation in der Deutschen Nationalbibliografie; detaillierte bibliografische Daten sind im Internet unter http://dnb.d-nb.de abrufbar.

Umschlagmotiv und -gestaltung: Olaf Schumacher
Satz und Layout: Andreas Paqué, www.paque.de
Printed in Czech Republic 2015
ISBN 978-3-7306-0208-9
www.anacondaverlag.de
info@anacondaverlag.de

A is for ...
wie ...

airy-fairy
Not strong, weak.
Larifari, luschige Einstellung

anal, anally retentive
Overly meticulous and zealous about even the most trivial things.
Übertrieben pingelig, pedantisch

an **anorak**
A person who is overly obsessed with intellectual or boring subjects (trainspotting, stamp collecting, computers, etc.)
Nerd; Jemand, der sich obsessiv mit seinem langweiligen Hobby beschäftigt (Briefmarken sammeln, etc.)

an **ape**
Often used to describe hairy or uncouth men.
Affe; ein stark behaarter oder ungepflegter Mann

arse
Slang term for the posterior.
Arsch

"He talks through his arse!"
Refers to people who don't know what they are talking about or simply tell lies.
"Der labert nur Scheiße!"

an **arse bandit**
A derogatory term for a homosexual.
Abfällige Bezeichnung für einen Schwulen

"Arse over tit" or **"arse over elbow"**
To fall over spectacularly. Example: "I fell arse over tit on the ice."
Auf die Fresse legen

an **arsehole**
The English version of probably the world's most famous insult.
Arschloch – Die englische Version des wohl berühmtesten Schimpfworts der Welt

arseholed
Extremely drunk.
Total besoffen, sternhagelvoll

an **arselicker**
A sycophant. Also known as "bootlicker".
Arschkriecher, Schleimer

an **arsewipe**
A thoroughly contemptible, detestable person.
Arschgeige

B is for …
wie …

a **backstabbing bastard**
A traitor.
(Hinterhältiger/mieser) Verräter

a **bag of shit**
A horrible person. Also someone who looks unkempt. "He looks like a bag of shit!"
Drecksack; auch: jemand, der vollkommen ungepflegt aussieht

bald as a coot
This means to be totally bald, to not have a single hair on your head.
Vollkommen kahl ("kahl wie ein Blesshuhn")

a **baldy**
A man with no hair.
Glatzkopf

a ballbreaker

A woman with serious men issues, who loves to destroy men's confidence and makes their lives a misery.

Eine Frau, die Männer klein hält und ihnen das Leben zur Hölle macht – ihnen "die Eier rausreißt"

"Balls!"

Literally this means "testicles". This expression is used in the same way as "bollocks", but usually to express frustration or disappointment.

"Scheiße!", "Mist!" (Wörtlich "Eier"/"Hoden", drückt Frustration oder Enttäuschung aus)

baloney (US)

Nonsense.

Quatsch, Unfug

bananas

Crazy. (Example: "He's gone bananas!")

Verrückt, durchgedreht

banged up

Pregnant or in prison.

Schwanger sein; im Knast sitzen

banging

Having sex.

Vögeln, bumsen

barking or barking mad

Totally crazy.

Vollkommen verrückt/bescheuert

barmy

Another term for "crazy".

Bekloppt

a **basket case**
Nice way of describing a slightly crazy person.
Spinner

a **bastard**
A "bastard" is a child born out of wedlock. Therefore this is one of the strongest insults you could use towards another person.
Ursprünglich: uneheliches Kind; heute universal anwendbar: Bastard, Dreckskerl, Schwein, Arschloch

a **battleaxe**
An old, usually grumpy woman who makes her husband's life a misery.
Hausdrachen

"Like a **beached whale!**"
This expression is used to describe overweight, obese people who are lying around. On a beach, for example.
Fette Kuh, Walross; beschreibt übergewichtige, korpulente Menschen

a **bellend**
A "bellend" is literally the end of a penis. Calling someone a "bellend" is a rather nasty way of saying you think they are an idiot.
Eigentlich: die Eichel; Idiot, Arschloch

"Belt up!"
"Be quiet!"
"Halt die Klappe!"

a **bender** (1)
A derogatory term for a male homosexual.
Schwuchtel

a **bender** (2), **to be on a bender**
A heavy drinking session.
Besäufnis, Sauferei, (Trink-)Gelage

bent
Homosexual or corrupt.
Schwul; korrupt

"As **bent as a boomerang!**"
Homosexual.
"Vom anderen Ufer", schwul

"As **bent as a nine-bob note!**"
Either very homosexual or very corrupt.
Extrem schwul bzw. korrupt

a **berk**
These days an inoffensive way of calling someone a bit of an idiot, although originally cockney rhyming slang for a rather more offensive insult (short for "Berkeley Hunt" – cunt).
Trottel

an (old) **biddy**
An old woman, especially a garrulous one.
Eine alte Schachtel, Tratschtante

"(You) **big baby!**"
Used in instances of cowardice or a reluctance to do something dangerous.
Angsthase, Feigling

a **big girl's blouse**
Unmanly, cowardly, wimpy man.
Ein Mann ohne Arsch in der Hose; feiger, erbärmlicher, devoter Ja-Sager

a **bighead**
An innocuous way of telling someone they are arrogant.
Angeber

a **bigot**
A person who is intolerantly obsessed with their own opinions and prejudices.
Intolerante Person, die nur ihre eigenen Ansichten gelten lässt

a **Billy bodge-it**
"(To) bodge" means to do a job quickly without any attention to detail. This is a put-down for a man who does such work around the home.
Pfuscher

a **Billy Bouffant**
Describes a man with a puffed-up bouffant hairstyle.
Jemand mit Toupierfrisur

a Billy no-mates
A great and popular expression describing yourself or someone who is alone, or appears to be unpopular or friendless.
Beliebter Ausdruck für einen Einzelgänger, der keine Freunde hat

a (blonde) bimbo
A stupid, usually blonde and attractive woman.
(Blondes) Dummchen, Häschen; eine dumme, meistens blonde und sehr attraktive Frau

a bint
Derogatory term for a woman.
Weibsbild

a birdbrain (also brain dead or brainless)
Stupid.
Spatzenhirn

bitchy
Nasty.
Gemein, gehässig

"You don't have to bite my head off!"
A retort to someone who over-reacts to an innocuous comment.
"Du musst mir nicht gleich den Kopf abreißen!"

biz
An old-fashioned word for "shit".
Scheiße (veraltet)

a blabbermouth
Someone with a big mouth who cannot keep a secret.
Plappermaul, Tratschtante

a blackleg
A strikebreaker. Someone who goes back to work while others are still protesting.
Streikbrecher (jemand, der trotz Streik zur Arbeit geht und die Kollegen im Stich lässt)

a blaggard
An unprincipled contemptible person. An untrustworthy person. Usually, only used to refer to a man.
Lump, gemeiner Mensch

"Bleedin' hell!"
Stronger form of "bloody hell!"
Steigerungsform von "bloody hell!" (siehe unten) – "Ach du Scheiße!"

"Little bleeder!"
A retort used to show anger or frustration towards someone.
"Du kleines Biest!"

a blighter
A rather posh way of referring to a man in an unfavourable way: "Just wait until I get my hands on that blighter!"
Nichtsnutz, Mistkerl

"(Cor) Blimey!"
Exclamation of shock or surprise. Often used in a light-hearted, overexaggerated manner to mean "I don't believe it!"
"Meine Güte!" (steht für "God blind me!")

"As blind as a bat."
Suffering from poor eyesight.
Blind wie ein Maulwurf

a blockhead
An idiot.
Holzkopf

"Blood and sand!"
A restrained expression of frustration, used as a mild form of "bloody hell!"
"Zum Donnerwetter!"; abgeschwächte Form von "bloody hell!"

"Bloody hell!"

The most famous and popular expression of dismay in the English language. Used to describe frustration, surprise or anger and can be used in all types of company.

"Ach du Scheiße!"; beliebtester Ausdruck, um z. B. Ärger, Frust, Überraschung oder Wut auszudrücken – universal einsetzbar

bloody-minded

Stubborn, obstinate. The term "pig-headed" can also be used to describe people like this.

Stur, dickköpfig

"Blooming heck!"

Very mild form of "bloody hell".

"Verflixt und zugenäht!"; harmlose Variante von "bloody hell!"

a **blow job** (also **giving head**)

A crude term for oral sex given to a man.

Derber Begriff für Oralsex

bog-eyed (also **boss-eyed, cross-eyed**)

A person who can't see straight and squints when they look at you.

Schielend

"Bog off!"

Friendly and innocuous way of telling someone to go away. ("Bog" is actually an everyday term for "toilet".)

"Hau ab!"

bog standard

Normal, nothing special.

08/15, nichts Besonderes

a bogey
What comes out of someone's nose if they pick it.
Popel

a bollock brain
An idiot.
Vollidiot

"Bollocks!"
Rubbish! Another way of forcefully telling someone "I don't believe you!"
Totaler Quatsch, Schwachsinn (wortwörtlich: Hoden, Eier). Deutliche Art und Weise jemandem zu sagen, dass man ihm nicht glaubt

bone idle
Terribly lazy.
Stinkfaul

a bonehead (US)
An idiot.
Idiot

a boner
An erect penis.
Ständer

bonkers
Crazy.
Übergeschnappt

bonking
A colloquial term for having sex.
Vögeln, bumsen

boobs
A colloquial term for breasts.
Titten, Möpse

a bootlicker
A sycophant. See also "arselicker".
Arschkriecher, Schleimer

a boozer
"Booze" is the colloquial term for alcohol. A boozer consumes lots of it. Also a pub.
Säufer; auch Kneipe

a frightful bore
A posh term for an extremely boring person.
Sterbenslangweilige Person

"Born with a silver spoon in their mouth."
Someone who is born into a rich, upper-class family who didn't have to work for what they've got.
Mit dem goldenen Löffel im Mund geboren sein; jemand, der nie einen Finger krumm machen musste

bossy boots
A name used by children to describe someone, usually a young girl, who likes to boss everyone around and take charge of everything.
Ein Kind (v. a. Mädchen), das sich aufspielt und alle anderen herumkommandiert

a **bottler**
To "have bottle" means to have nerve or to be courageous. A bottler has neither of these attributes.
Feigling, Memme

a **bozo** (US)
An idiot or fool. Dumb.
Idiot, Dummkopf

brassed off
Mild form of "pissed off".
Harmloser Ausdruck für "angepisst sein"

"Built like a **brick shithouse.**"
This is a term used to describe someone, usually a man, who is strong, big and muscular.
Ein Mann, der extrem groß und stark gebaut ist

bristols

A colloquial term for breasts. From cockney rhyming slang "Bristol City – Titty".

Titten

a **brownnoser**

A sycophant.

Arschkriecher

a **bugger**

Although this is an extremely rude word (the term "(to) bugger" actually means to sodomise someone), it's used as a very mild insult and can sometimes be used as a term of endearment. For example, you can call a small child, in an affectionate way, "a little bugger!"

Obwohl "to bugger" ein sehr vulgärer Ausdruck ist (es bedeutet eigentlich "jemanden in den Arsch ficken"), wird er in einem herzlichen Kontext verwendet: "der kleine Stinker/Scheißer!" (Kind)

"Bugger all!"

Nothing.

Überhaupt nichts, rein gar nichts

"Bugger it!"

"Damn!"

"Verdammt!"

"Bugger me!"

No, it doesn't mean "sodomise me", but "I don't believe it!"

"Ich fass' es nicht!"

"Bugger off!"

Very mild form of "piss off!" ("go away!")

"Verzieh' dich!"

buggered
In a bad situation.
In Schwierigkeiten sein, am Arsch sein

"Bull!" or **"Bullshit!"**
Nonsense.
"Unsinn!", "Quatsch!"

a **bullshitter**
A person who speaks nonsense or tells lies to enhance their own reputation.
Jemand, der permanent Mist erzählt oder Lügen verbreitet, um sich aufzuspielen

a **bummer**
A derogatory term for a male homosexual.
Schwuchtel

"What a bummer!"
An expression of regret or sorrow. (Example: "You've lost your job? What a bummer!")
"So ein Mist!"

a (country) **bumpkin**
A simple person, usually from a rural background.
Hinterwäldler, Landei

a **busybody**
A person who is always making a fuss about things unnecessarily, or interferes in other people's business.
Wichtigtuer; jemand, der unnötig Dinge aufbauscht oder sich in Sachen einmischt, die ihn nichts angehen

butch
A masculine woman.
Maskulin; maskuline Frau

butt (US)
Bottom.
Arsch, Hintern

"Butter wouldn't melt in his/her mouth."
Innocent. Often used sarcastically to describe an unpleasant, underhand or dishonest person.
"Er/sie sieht aus, als könne er/sie kein Wässerchen trüben"; abfällig für jemanden, der das Unschuldslamm spielt

butterfingers
Someone who always drops or mishandles things.
Tollpatsch

"Butt out!"
"Mind your own business!"
"Kümmere dich um deinen eigenen Kram!"

"Button it!"
"Shut up!"
"Halt den Mund!"

C is for ... wie ...

cack-handed
Clumsy or left-handed.
Ungeschickt

a **call girl**
A prostitute.
Nutte

"Don't call us, we'll call you!"
A nice way of telling someone you are unimpressed with whatever they might be offering.
Eine freundliche Absage, z. B. bei Bewerbungen: "Wir melden uns bei Ihnen!"

a **carthorse**
An extremely slow person.
Trantüte

a **chav**
A modern-day term for white trash (US), lower class (GB).
Proll

cheap
Miserly.
Geizig, knauserig

a **cheapskate**
A person who does not part with their money easily.
Geizkragen

cheeky
Often used to describe misbehaving children who answer adults back.
Vorlaut, frech

cheesed off
A very mild form of "pissed off".
Angeödet

a **chicken**
Afraid. Not brave.
Angsthase

"As much use as a chocolate teapot."
A popular expression to describe someone who is useless.
Beliebter Ausdruck für jemanden, der zu nichts zu gebrauchen ist

clever clogs (also a **clever Dick**)
A term used to mock someone who attempts to appear intelligent.
Klugscheißer

a **clit**
A short, rather crude form of the word 'clitoris'.
Kitzler; geschmacklose Kurzform für Klitoris

a **clot**
A fool.
Dummkopf, Trottel, Depp

cloth ears
This expression describes people who haven't heard what you've said.
Taube Nuss

"Living in cloud cuckoo land"
A wonderful expression to describe someone who is detached from reality.
Hinterm Mond leben

"Cobblers!"
Another form of the expression "bollocks!" This expression basically means you do not believe a single word the other person is saying. Cockney rhyming slang "Cobbler's awl" – ball.
"Unsinn! Erzähl keinen Scheiß!" (wortwörtlich: Hoden, Eier)

cock happy
A derogatory term used by men to describe a woman who likes sex.
Sexgeil (abfällige Beschreibung einer Frau, die gerne und viel Sex hat)

a **cock-up**
A complete mess. A disaster from start to finish.
Schlamassel, ein totales Desaster

cocky
Incredibly self-assured.
Eingebildet

an old **codger**
A term usually reserved for grumpy old men.
Alter Knacker

"Codswallop!"
A mild form of "bullshit".
"So ein Käse!"; Stuss

a con artist (also confidence trickster)
A fraud, a swindler. A person who cheats people out of money by unscrupulous means.
Schwindler, Hochstapler

"You conning git!"
"You cheat!"
"Du mieser Betrüger!"

a copper's nark (also a grass)
A police informer.
Polizeispitzel

corny
Sentimental, trite or banal. Also used to describe old jokes or puns. ("That's really corny.")
Kitschig, abgedroschen. Auch im Kontext von alten Witzen ("Kalauer")

a couch potato
A lazy person who spends most of their time on the couch in front of the TV.
Stubenhocker, der nur vor der Glotze hängt

a cowardly custard
An old-fashioned children's term to describe someone who is afraid of doing something.
Angsthase (veraltet, Kindersprache)

a cradle snatcher
An older person who has a much younger partner (literally seen as "snatching the baby" from the cradle).
Ältere Person mit deutlich jüngerem Partner (wortwörtlich "Kindesräuber/in")

"You crafty beggar/sod/mare!"
Used in response to underhand, secretive or sly behaviour.
"Du gewiefter Hund!", "Du hinterhältiges Schwein!"

a crank (US)
A crazy, possibly psychopathic person.
Spinner

crap; crappy
A milder variation of "shit" or "shitty".
Scheiß; beschissen (etwas weniger vulgär als "shit/shitty")

having a crap (also: **having a dump, having a shit**)
Crude terms for moving your bowels.
Kacken

"Everything has gone down the crapper!"
Everything has gone wrong.
"Das ist alles scheiße gelaufen!", "alles geht den Bach runter"

a **crawler**
A sycophant. Someone who seeks favour (usually from superiors) by being over-friendly, helpful or complimentary.
Arschkriecher, Schleimer

a **creep; creepy**
Usually used by women to describe a man they don't like, someone who is over-friendly, forward or intimate. It can also be used to describe someone who seeks the favour of their superiors by being sycophantic.
Fieser Typ, Schleimer; gruselig

a **cretin**
Someone who you think is an absolute fool.
Schwachkopf

"Crikey!"
A very mild and inoffensive expression of surprise.
"Wow!", "Meine Güte!", "Ach herrje!" (überraschter Ausruf)

a **crock of shit**
A lot of nonsense. Bullshit.
Ein Haufen Unsinn

crumpet
Male, macho term for attractive women. (Example: "Was there a lot of crumpet at the party?")
Bräute, Ischen, Tussis

a **crybaby**
Over-emotional, crying at the littlest thing.
Heulsuse

D is for ... wie ...

"As daft as a brush"

A gentle way of saying that someone is a little bit stupid.
So schlau wie zehn Meter Feldweg

a **daft cow**

A comment exclusively used as an insult for women.
Blöde Kuh

a **dago**

A derogatory term for a Spaniard or Italian.
Abwertender Begriff für Spanier und Italiener; Spaniockel, Itaker

"Damn!"

Exclamation expressing anger or frustration.
"Verdammt!"

daylight robbery

A total rip off. A ridiculous price for something.
Abzocke, Wucher

"Dead from the neck up!"

Stupid.
Hirnlos

a **dead leg**

A useless, lazy person.
Hänger, Faulenzer

a **deadbeat**

A dull, lazy, unreliable person.
Faulpelz, Taugenichts

"As **deaf as a post**." (Also "As **deaf as a doornail**.")

Used to describe old people who are hard of hearing or used in exasperation when people haven't heard what's been said.
"Taub wie eine Nuss", stocktaub

"(They're suffering from) delusions of grandeur!"
This refers to people who see themselves as far more important or brilliant than they actually are in reality.
Größenwahnsinnig, überheblich

dense
Stupid.
Dumm

"The devil farts in my face again!"
An expression of bitter disappointment or frustration.
"Ich habe wieder die Arschkarte gezogen!"; Ausdruck, wenn man wieder mal Pech gehabt hat.

a **dick/a dickhead**
Another impolite way of telling someone that you are not very impressed with them. "Dick" is a colloquial word for penis, referring to someone in this way leaves them in no doubt how you feel about them.
Schwanz, Arschloch

a **dildo**
An artificial penis-shaped object used for female masturbation. This expression can also be used to describe a stupid person.
Dildo; auch als Beleidigung

a dimwit
An idiot. A stupid person.
Dummkopf, Vollidiot

a dingbat
An inoffensive term to describe someone who is a bit of a fool.
Trottel

a dinosaur
An old-fashioned person. Someone who is out of date and who is living in the past or belongs to a bygone age.
Jemand von gestern, Betonkopf

dipping one's wick (also **getting one's end away**)
A humorous term for a man having sex.
Seinen Schwanz reinstecken

dippy
Not sensible, foolish.
Übergeschnappt

a dipstick
A very mild form of calling someone an idiot.
Dummkopf (harmlos)

a dirtbag (US)
A scumbag, the lowest of the low.
Drecksack

a dirty bastard
This can be used to describe a pervert, or a tenacious football player.
Perversling, aber auch ein nicht unterzukriegender, zäher Fußballspieler

dirty minded
Perverted.
Versaut, eine schmutzige Fantasie haben

a dirty old man (also **a lech**, **a lecher** or **lecherous**)
An older male who leers after young girls or attractive women.
Alter Lüstling

ditzy
Foolish, stupid.
Doof

a **diva**

A headstrong woman who thinks it's her divine right to get whatever she wants and to behave in any way she wants to.

Diva

a **dive**

A dirty club or pub, usually frequented by undesirables.

Spelunke

a **divvy**

An idiot.

Idiot

dizzy

Idiotic.

Dusselig

dodgy

A questionable person, thing or situation. The origins of this might possibly come from the Charles Dickens' character "the Artful Dodger".

Beschreibt eine zwielichtige Person oder eine heikle Situation. Der Begriff geht wahrscheinlich auf Charles Dickens' Protagonisten "the Artful Dodger" aus "Oliver Twist" zurück.

a **dog** (or **dog rough**)

An ugly woman.

Schreckschraube

dog breath

Bad breath, usually the morning after going out on the piss; a person whose breath smells bad.

Mundgeruch

a **dog's body**

A person who does all the hard work (usually for other people).

Sklave, Handlanger, der die ganze schwere Arbeit für andere erledigt

"The dog's bollocks!"

Literally means "the dog's testicles", but in this case it means "fantastic!"

Wörtlich "die Hoden des Hundes", hier jedoch: "fantastisch!"

"She's dressed up like a dog's dinner!"

A "bitchy" insult, usually traded between women who don't particularly like each other.

"Die sieht vielleicht billig aus!" (Meist eine Beleidigung zwischen Frauen, die sich auf den Tod nicht ausstehen können)

"Like a dog with two dicks!"
Extremely happy.
Extrem glücklich

a donkey
A slow person. Often used to describe footballers whose talent or speed might be questionable.
Lahme Ente

a doofus
An incompetent, foolish, or stupid person.
Idiot, Blödmann

a dope; dopey
Forgetful or lackadaisical person.
Trottel, Dumpfbacke, Trantüte; vergesslich und lasch

a dopey mare
A milder version of "dozy cow".
Noch harmloser als "dusselige Kuh"

a dork
A stupid or inept person. Similar to "geek".
Depp, Trottel

a dosser
A useless person. Usually someone who sits around lazily. Can also be used to describe a tramp or homeless person.
Penner, Faulenzer; wird auch für Landstreicher oder Obdachlose verwendet

a dosshouse
Old term used to describe a cheap form of accommodation. Now used to describe a place which is untidy and where anyone can stay over, in any particular place (on the floor, in the kitchen, etc.)
Billige Absteige

a dozy bint
A dozy or forgetful woman.
Eine trantütige oder vergessliche Frau

a dozy cow
"You dozy cow" is a friendly way of reprimanding a woman for being a little bit forgetful.
Dusselige Kuh

"They look like they've been dragged through a hedge backwards."

Used to describe untidy, unkempt people.

Umschreibung für ungepflegte Leute: "Die sehen aus, als wären sie rückwärts durch die Hecke gezogen worden."

a **dragon**

An old woman, more often than not a mother-in-law, who makes other people's lives a misery.

(Haus-)Drache, Hexe; wird gerne für alte Frauen oder Schwiegermütter verwendet, die einem das Leben zur Hölle machen

a **drama queen**

A person, more often than not a young woman or girl (but can also be used for men), who makes a drama out of the most innocuous situations.

Drama-Queen, hysterische Tussi

the dregs (of society)

The lowest level of society. Usually reserved for criminals or other lowlife.

Abschaum

a drip

"You drip!" is a nice way of reprimanding someone for a minor slip-up.

Tollpatsch

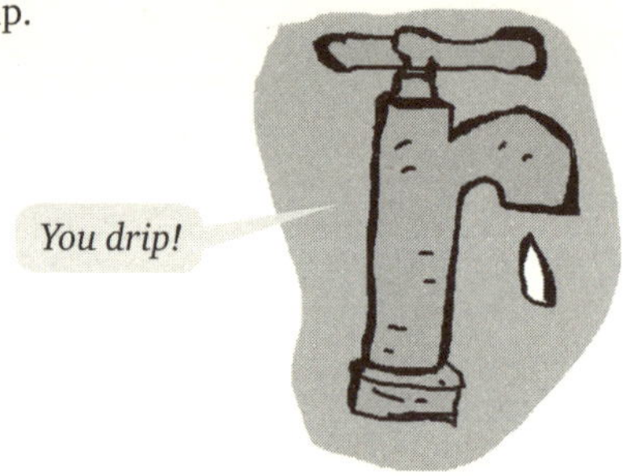

drivel

Nonsense.

Blödsinn

"Drop dead!"

Another way of telling someone to go away.

"Verpiss dich!"

dropping your guts (also letting rip, letting one drop, cutting the cheese)

Colloquial terms for farting.

Einen fahren lassen, furzen

looking like a **drowned rat**
Extremely wet.
Pudelnass

a **drufford**
A drunk. Someone who drinks excessively.
Säufer

a **druggie**
An undesirable person who is suspected of being a drug user.
Junkie

"Dry up!"
"Shut up!"
"Halt's Maul!"

a **duffer**
"Duff" means useless. A "duffer" therefore is a useless person.
Niete

a **dullard**
A slow-witted person.
Dummkopf

dumb
Stupid.
Dumm

a **dumbass**
A stupid person.
Vollpfosten, Dumpfbacke

a **dumbo**
A person regarded as stupid.
Blödian

a **dunce**
An idiot, especially academically.
Dummkopf, v. a. schlechter Schüler

E is for ...
wie ...

an **eejit**
The Scottish and Irish version of "idiot".
Schottische und irische Version von "Idiot"

effing and blinding

Colloquial term for swearing/using very bad language.
*Fluchen; "effing" steht für f***ing, also "fucking", "blinding" für "blimey"/"God blind me!"*

"Effing hell!"

This is the non-swearing version of "fucking hell!"
"Scheibenkleister!"

an **egghead**

A mild term to describe a person who is considered intellectually gifted in the field of academics (also "boffin").
Eierkopf, Schlaumeier (abwertend gegenüber einem Intellektuellen)

an **Essex girl**

This is like a regional version of a blonde bimbo, which applies to a female seen as overly promiscuous and unintelligent, characteristics attributed to women from the county of Essex.
Dummes Flittchen; Bezeichnung für promiskuitive und dümmliche Frauen – Charaktereigenschaften, die Frauen aus der Region Essex zugeschrieben werden

"Excuse my French."

This expression is an indispensable aid for someone who wishes to swear or is about to swear. It can be used before or after the expletive.
"Entschuldigen Sie meine Ausdrucksweise!" (Vor oder nach dem Fluchen gebraucht, um sich zu entschuldigen, aber gleichzeitig auch um zu signalisieren, dass man noch viel mehr schimpfen könnte)

F is for …
wie …

"F off!"

Non-swearing version of "fuck off".
"Verpiss dich!" (abgeschwächte Variante von "fuck off")

"He's got a **face I'd love to slap!**"

Normally refers to men who wear self-satisfied smiles on their faces at all times.
"Der hat ein Gesicht zum Reinschlagen!"

"A face like a slapped arse!"

Not a pretty sight.
Arschgesicht

(to) **faff/fanny** around

To put a lot of effort into doing nothing.
Rumtrödeln

a **faggot/a fag** (US)

Unpleasant term for a homosexual.
Schwuchtel

a **fairy**

A disparaging term for a homosexual or effeminate male.
Tunte

(Mr.) fancy pants
Pretentious, overly sophisticated. Someone who is dressed fancy or acts in a fancy matter (sometimes used with a "Mr." prefix).
Schickimicki

fanny
A mild colloquial word for vagina.
Muschi, Möse

(to) **fart**
To break wind.
Furzen

an **old fart**
A staid or boring man, also known as "boring old fart".
Langweiler

a **fathead**
A stupid person.
Dummkopf

fatso (or **fatty**)
Disparaging description of an overweight person.
Fettsack, Fettwanst

fellatio
The art of performing oral sex on a male.
Einem Mann einen blasen

a **fibber**
A liar.
Lügner, Schwindler, Aufschneider

"He couldn't **fight his way out of a paper bag.**"
Terribly puny or weak.
Schwächling; extrem mickrig oder schwach

the filth (also the **pigs**, the **scum**, the **old Bill**, the **cops** and the **fuzz**)

Derogatory terms for the police.
Bullenschweine

filthy-minded

Tending to have vulgar, obscene, or lewd thoughts.
Versaut, eine schmutzige Fantasie haben

a **fink** (also **ratfink**)

A contemptible person.
Miese Ratte

(to) **fire blanks**

Sterile, unable to father a child.
Wörtlich: "mit Platzpatronen schießen"; impotent

flaky

Unreliable.
Unzuverlässig, verpeilt

Flash Harry

A man who likes to dress and behave in a flamboyant way.
Lackaffe; ein Mann, der sich extravagant kleidet und benimmt

"Don't **flatter** yourself!"

A great retort for someone who thinks they are more popular/attractive than they actually are.
"Bild' dir ja nichts ein!" (als Entgegnung, wenn jemand denkt, er ist der tollste Mensch auf Erden)

"Like **flies round shit**!"

A collective insult for a bunch of people who are taking a very close look at something interesting, or congregating around an attractive woman.
Wie die Fliegen um die Scheiße kreisen

a **floozy**

A loose woman of low morals.
Flittchen

fly-by-night

Not reliable or responsible, especially in business; untrustworthy. (Example: a fly-by-night operation.)
Nicht vertrauenswürdig, dubios (z. B. Nacht-und-Nebel-Aktion)

a fool
A stupid person.
Dummkopf, Narr

"A fool and his money are easily parted."
An apt expression describing someone who has been easily duped.
"Dummheit und Geld lassen sich nicht vereinen." Ein Ausdruck für jemanden, der sich leicht übers Ohr hauen lässt

"For Pete's sake!"
Milder version of "for fuck's sake!"
"Um Himmels willen!"

foul-mouthed
Constantly peppering one's speech with crude swearwords.
Bei jeder Gelegenheit Schimpfworte benutzend, vulgär

a four-letter word
A polite term for a swearword.
Schimpfwort (wie z. B. "fuck")

"Frankly my dear, I don't give a damn!"
A great put-down for someone who is trying to get the better of you. (Quote from "Gone with the Wind").
"Offen gesagt, pfeif' ich drauf." (Zitat aus "Vom Winde verweht")

a freak

A strange person.
Freak (wörtlich: Missgeburt)

a freeloader

A person who likes to drink at other people's expense.
Schnorrer; jemand, der gerne auf Kosten anderer trinkt

"Frig off!"

Somewhere between "bugger off" and "sod off".
"Verzieh' dich!"

"Friggin' hell!"

Somewhere between "bloody hell" and "bleedin' hell".
"Verdammt noch mal!"

a Frog (or Froggie)

A person from France. (No doubt derived from the French preference for frogs' legs.)
Franzose (ganz klar, wegen der Vorliebe der Franzosen für Froschschenkel)

a fruitcake

A crazy or eccentric person.
Spinner, Exzentriker

fuck

The mother verb/noun for so many of its offspring.
Ficken, Fick, Scheiße; das Urschimpfwort (Verb und Substantiv), das es in unzähligen Variationen gibt

"Fuck it!"

Normally used in instances of frustration or resignation.
"Ach, scheiße!" (vor allem in Momenten der Frustration und Resignation)

"Fuck off!"

The most famous swearword of all time? The archetypal four-letter word.
"Verpiss dich!", "Leck mich am Arsch!" – das berühmteste Schimpfwort aller Zeiten?

"Fuck you!"

Definitely not an invitation to have sex with someone!
Garantiert keine Einladung zum Sex – "fick dich!"

"Go (and) **fuck** yourself!"

A categorical "no!"
"Fick dich!"

"For **fuck's** sake!"

Another expression of total exasperation.
Noch eine Variante des F-Worts, um seinen ganzen Frust auszudrücken. "Verdammt noch mal!", "So 'ne Scheiße!"

"Get **fucked!**"

A variation of "fuck yourself!"
"Fick dich!"

a **fucker**

Nasty person, someone you definitely don't have time for.
Arschloch

fuckface

Nasty insult.
Arschgesicht

"Fucking hell!"
The hardcore version of "bloody hell!"
"Verdammte Scheiße!"

a **fuckwit**
A total fool.
Vollidiot, Flachwichser

a **fusspot**
Someone who is always making a fuss about nothing.
Umstandskrämer

G is for … wie …

"Gagging for it!"
A derogatory, unkind and macho term used by men to describe women who might or might not be desperate for sex.
Macho-Redewendung: "Die bettelt ja nur drum, flachgelegt zu werden!"

a **gannet**
A greedy person.
Gierhals, Vielfraß

a **gasbag**
A person who talks too much.
Quasselstrippe

a geek
A non-mainstream person, usually intellectual and unattractive. An outsider obsessed with boring things like mathematics or computer technology.
Streber, Computerfreak, Nerd – intelligenter aber meistens unattraktiver Außenseiter mit Spezialwissen auf einem nicht massentauglichen Gebiet wie z. B. Mathe

"(Did you) get out of bed on the wrong side?"
A question asked to someone who is in a bad mood, or grumpy.
"Bist du heute morgen mit dem linken Fuß aufgestanden?"

a gibbering wreck
An extremely nervous person.
Nervenbündel

a git
A semi-nasty way of telling someone you don't really like them. ("You're a git!")
Depp, Blödmann

"Give it a rest!"
Exasperated way of asking someone to be quiet.
"Halt mal die Luft an!"

"Give me strength!"
Another (non-swearing) mild term to express frustration.
"Nur ruhig bleiben!"

a glorified gofer
A term describing someone who has a job which they think is far more important than it actually is. ("Go for this, go for that …")
Wichtigtuer

a glutton
Someone who overeats or eats like a pig.
Fresssack, Vielfraß

"Go and boil your head!"
A rather direct way of informing someone what they can do with themselves.
Eine weitere deutliche Aufforderung an jemanden, sich zu verpissen

"Go and take a running jump!"
"Go away!"
"Hau ab!"

"Go to hell!"

"Go away", "leave me alone" or "damn you"!
"Fahr' zur Hölle!", "Scher' dich zum Teufel!"

gobbledygook

Nonsense. (Example: "He's talking gobbledygook!")
Kauderwelsch

gobby

Loud-mouthed.
Großmäulig

a **gobshite**

"Gob" is a colloquial term for "spit", "shite" is another word for "shit". "A gobshite" is someone who is full of shit and doesn't mind letting the world know it.
Klugscheißer

a **gold digger**

A derogatory term for a young woman who wants an older man for his money.
Eine Frau, die nur aufs Geld aus ist

"He's gone to the dogs."
(Also "gone to seed".)

Deteriorated.
"Er ist vor die Hunde gegangen."

"Good for nothing!"
Self-explanatory put-down.
"Zu nichts zu gebrauchen!"

"Good riddance to bad rubbish!"
A derogatory farewell to someone you don't like.
"Gut, dass ich den los bin!"

goolies
Testicles.
Eier, Klöten

a goon
An old-fashioned way of calling someone an idiot.
Dummkopf (altmodisch)

"Gordon Bennett!"
No one is quite sure why this name is used to show total exasperation.
"Du meine Güte!", "Heiliger Bimbam!"

gormless
Inoffensively stupid.
Dämlich

a greaseball
A person with greasy hair, especially one of Mediterranean or Latin American origin.
Schmieriger Typ (insbesondere aus Südamerika oder dem Mittelmeerraum)

"The great unwashed."
Lower class people.
Unterschicht

"Green behind the ears."
Naïve.
Grün hinter den Ohren, naiv

gross (US)
Disgusting.
Widerlich

grotty
Dirty and cheap. Mostly used to describe buildings, especially clubs, pubs or homes.
Heruntergekommen, versifft (v. a. Gebäude)

"Grow up!" (Also **"Act your age!"**)
A put-down for someone who is behaving childishly.
"Werd' erwachsen!"

gutless
Cowardly.
Feige, keine Eier haben

gutted
Extremely disappointed.
Total enttäuscht

a **guttersnipe**
An old expression meaning street urchin, a person of the lowest class.
Gassenjunge, Göre (veraltet)

"I hate your **guts!**"
To really despise someone.
Jemanden wie die Pest hassen ("guts" bedeutet eigentlich "Eingeweide")

a greedy **guts**
Someone who eats a lot, and quickly, and is not particularly bothered if other people get their share.
Vielfraß

"Grumpy **guts!**"
A way to tell somebody they are being bad tempered or miserable.
"Du Miesepeter!"

a **gyppo**
An unpleasant reference to a gypsy. This label is given, sometimes rather unfairly, to most people in Britain who travel around in caravans: new age travellers, fairground owners, etc.
Zigeuner

H is for …
wie …

a **half-wit**
A foolish or stupid person.
Schwachkopf

hanky panky
A humorous term for having sex.
Techtelmechtel

a hardcase
A tough, often violent male.
Schlägertyp

a hard-on
A sexually aroused male gets "a hard-on".
Ständer, Latte

"Has someone stolen your crayons?"
A great put-down for someone behaving in an immature or childish manner.
"Na, hat dir jemand dein Spielzeug weggenommen?"

having it off/away
Having sex.
Es treiben

a headbanger
A crazy person. Could also refer to someone shaking their head violently to heavy metal music.
Irrer; jemand, der auf Heavy Metal abgeht

a headcase
A crazy person.
Spinner, Bekloppter

a headless chicken
A brainless person, someone who acts without thinking, usually dashing around in a panicked way.
Aufgescheuchtes Huhn

a head-the-ball (Scottish: **heid-the-baw**)
A bit of an idiot.
Spinner

heavy petting
Sexual relations that do not include penetration.
Petting

"Hell fire!"
Blasphemous version of "bloody hell!"
"Verdammte Scheiße!", "Zum Teufel!"

a **hellraiser**
A person who thrives on behaving badly or causing trouble for others.
Unruhestifter

a **hippie**
A name given to anyone over 40 who has long hair and doesn't wear "normal" clothes.
Hippie (allgemein jeder über 40 mit langen Haaren und alternativen Klamotten)

a **homo**
A derogatory term for a gay man.
Homo, Schwuchtel

a **honkey**
Black man's term for a white man.
Abwertende Bezeichnung für einen Weißen

Hooray Henry
An upper class male from a privileged background. More often than not toffee-nosed, arrogant and aloof.
Lärmender arroganter Oberschicht-Schnösel

"How's your father?"
An old, rather quaint term for having sex. (Example: "Do you fancy a little bit of how's your father?")
Eine drollige Umschreibung für Sex

(to) get the **hump**
To become angry or annoyed with someone.
Auf jemanden wütend werden

humping
Another everyday word for having sex.
Bumsen

I is for … / wie …

an idiot

Internationally-known insult. Only the pronunciation differs from country to country.

Wer kennt diesen Ausdruck nicht? Nur die Aussprache variiert von Land zu Land.

"If he had a brain, he'd be dangerous!"

Bringing someone's intelligence into question.

"Nur gut, dass er nichts im Kopf hat!"

an ignoramus

An old-fashioned word meaning a stupid idiot.

Dummkopf, Ignorant (veraltet)

an imbecile

A total idiot.

Schwachkopf, Idiot

J is for … / wie …

"Jack shit!"

Nothing. Example: "What did you learn from that experience? – Jack shit!"

Rein gar nichts

a Jack-the-lad

A male who sees himself as a bad boy. A guy who walks about thinking he owns everything and loves attention.

Schmalspurganove, Prahlhans

a Jaffa

In British slang this means a man who has a low sperm count. A Jaffa is an orange that is seedless (hence the name).

Unfruchtbarer Mann – sein Sperma hat so wenig Samen wie eine kernlose Jaffa-Orange

jailbait

Young, underage, sexually provocative females, whose attentions could lead to an unwanted jail sentence for the man!
Lolita; attraktive Minderjährige, von der man besser die Finger lässt, wenn man nicht im Knast landen will

a **jailbird**

A person who has spent some time in prison or stands a good chance of ending up there in the future.
Knastbruder

a **jammy beggar**

Someone who is extremely lucky.
Glückspilz

a **jerk; (to) jerk off** (US)

A "jerk" is an American term for an idiot. "To jerk off" means to masturbate. (This can also be used to describe a person: "He's a total jerk-off!")
Wichser; wichsen

jerry-built

A disparaging term for a building/thing that has not been built very well.
Schlampig gebaut, gepfuscht

a (Southern) **Jessy**

A cowardly or ineffectual male.
Feigling (v. a. in Nordengland gebräuchlich)

"Jog on!"
A put-down for a woman to repel the unwanted advances of a man.
"Zieh' Leine!" (vor allem als Abfuhr an aufdringliche Männer)

John Thomas
An old-fashioned term for the penis.
Johannes (altmodisch für Penis)

a **johnnie**
A slang term for a condom.
Gummi, Kondom

jumped up
Snobby, arrogant.
Abgehoben, arrogant

K is for … wie …

the **kettle calling the pot black**
This expression is used when someone is being hypocritical. (Example: "You think I drink too much? Well, there's the kettle calling the pot black!")
"Ein Esel schimpft den anderen Langohr"; "das sagt der/die Richtige!"

a **kick in the teeth**
An expression of bitterness or disappointment, a let-down. (Example: "When he said he didn't want my help, it was like a kick in the teeth!")
Ein Schlag ins Gesicht/in die Fresse

a **killjoy**
Someone who wants to ruin other people's fun.
Spaßbremse, Spielverderber

kinky
Sexually perverted.
Pervers

"Kiss my arse!"
Another classic which leaves the recipient in no doubt as to where they stand with you.
"Leck mich am Arsch!"; Klassiker, der sehr deutlich macht, was man von jemandem hält

knackered

This means either extremely tired ("I'm knackered!"), or broken ("the fridge is knackered!")

Fix und fertig, kaputt

"Don't get your knickers in a twist!"

A nice expression asking someone not to get too upset or angry about something.

"Reg dich nicht auf!"

a **knob**

Crude term for penis.

Schwanz, Pimmel

a **knobhead**

Another version of "dickhead" – "knob" being a vulgar word to describe the male appendage.

Arschloch

knocked up

Pregnant.

Schwanger

knockers

Breasts.

Titten

a **knocking shop**

A place where people go to have sex. This could be a brothel, or a pub or club renowned as a meeting point for people looking for sex.

Bordell, Bumslokal, Abschleppkneipe

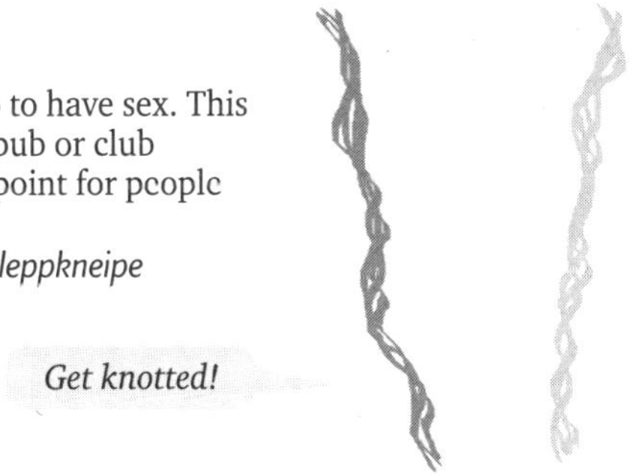

"Get knotted!"

Another harmless way of telling someone you are not impressed.

"Rutsch mir den Buckel runter!"

a **know-all**

An annoying person who thinks they know everything.

Besserwisser, Klugscheißer

a **knucklehead** (US)
A fool.
Schwachkopf

a **Kraut**
Unkind word to describe a German. (Probably derived from the Germans' love of sauerkraut.)
Ein/e Deutsche/r

L is for ... wie ...

la-di-da
Acting or talking in a false and annoying way that is thought to be typical of rich and important people.
Affektiert

(to) get **laid**
To have sex.
Vögeln, sich flachlegen lassen

a **lamebrain**
A fool.
Spatzenhirn

a **lardarse**
Lard is a white substance taken from the fat of animals, used for cooking. A "lardarse" would have a huge amount of this around their buttocks.
Fettarsch

a **layabout**
A person who literally lays around the place, doing very little.
Faulenzer, Gammler

a **lazy bones**
A person who doesn't move a muscle if they can help it.
Faulpelz

(to) get your leg over
A crude term for a man getting sex. (Example: “Did you get your leg over?”)
Drüberrutschen, flachlegen (Bsp.: “Hast du sie flachgelegt?”)

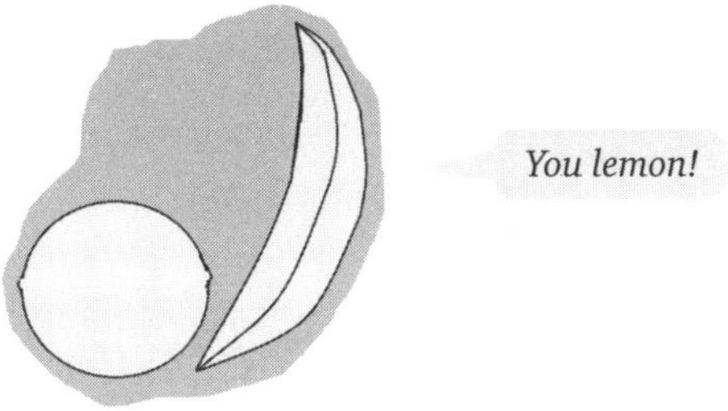

a **lemon**
An idiot.
Trottel

lesbo
A nasty term for a lesbian.
Abwertend für Lesbe

lily-livered
Cowardly.
Feige

a **limey**
An Englishman (as described by the Australians and Americans. Deriving from the use of limes to stave off scurvy aboard ships).
Engländer (amerikanischer/australischer Begriff; ursprünglich waren britische Seeleute gemeint, die, um Skorbut vorzubeugen, Zitrusfrüchte verzehrten)

limp-wristed
Effeminate, girly, possibly gay.
Tuntig

a **little Hitler**
A very politically incorrect way of describing someone who is overly bossy, or lets authority go to their head.
Politisch unkorrekt: eine rechthaberische Person als kleinen Hitler zu bezeichnen

a **loafer**
A lazy person.
Gammler, Faulenzer

a **loony bin**
An unkind term for a lunatic asylum.
Klapse

a loose woman
A woman seen as having low moral standards who may or may not sleep around.
Ein leichtes Mädchen

a loser
A mocking term to wind up a rival or opponent.
Verlierer, Versager

a loudmouth
A person with a lot to say for themselves, usually about themselves and their opinions.
Großmaul, Maulheld

a louse
A terrible person, lowest of the low.
Laus, miese Ratte

a (lager) lout
A "lout" is an uncouth, unruly youth (usually male). A "lager lout" is the beer-swilling, drunken version of this horrid specimen. (Lager is what the British call any kind of light-coloured imported beer.)
Rüpel, besoffener Rowdy (Lager: helles Bier)

a lush (also: a soak)
A heavy drinker.
Säufer

M is for … wie …

macho
A derisory term for an overly aggressive, sexist and masculine male.
Machomäßig

mad or "as mad as a hatter"
Crazy.
Verrückt, total durchgeknallt – wie der verrückte Hutmacher aus "Alice im Wunderland"

a maggot
A despicable person with no morals.
Made

male chauvinist pig (MCP)

A male who thinks women are merely objects to be used for pleasure or labour. A total sexist.

Chauvinistenschwein

a **malingering bastard**

"(To) malinger" means to drag out an illness as long as possible in order to delay going back to work.

Mieser Simulant

manky

Dirty, sticky, horrible.

Eklig, widerlich

a **mard-arse**

Old-fashioned term for a crybaby.

Heulsuse (veraltet)

a **meathead**

A stupid person.

Dummkopf

Mickey Mouse

Laughable, risible, cheap, not to be taken seriously. Example: "This is a bit Mickey Mouse."

Lachhaft, auf Kindergartenniveau

a **milksop**
A weak or ineffectual person.
Weichei, Milchbubi

"So what first attracted you to your **millionaire husband?"**
A subtle put-down for a suspected gold digger.
"Na, was hat dir an deinem Millionär als erstes gefallen?"

a **miser**
A penny pincher. Someone who does not like to spend money.
Geizhals, Pfennigfuchser

a **misery guts**
An incredibly bad-tempered, humourless person.
Griesgram

"Stop **mithering** me!"
(To) mither means to constantly annoy someone.
"Geh mir nicht auf die Nerven!"

a **moaner** (or a **moaning Minnie**)
Someone who complains a lot.
Miesepeter

a **moneygrabber**
A person only interested in their own financial gain.
Geldgieriger Mensch, Raffzahn

a **mong**
A cruel children's jibe. (The short form of the word "mongoloid".)
Behinderter, Mongo (Kurzform von "Mongoloide", abwertend)

a **moody bastard/bitch**
Male and female versions to describe someone with acute mood swings.
Jemand, der anderen mit seinen Stimmungsschwankungen auf die Nerven geht

a **moron**
An idiot. Completely stupid.
Vollidiot

a **motormouth**
Someone who talks rapidly, non-stop.
Quasselstrippe

a **muckraker**
Very similar to a "shit-stirrer". Someone who enjoys causing trouble.
Unruhestifter, Schmierfink (Reporter)

a mudslinger
A person who throws insults around indiscriminately.
Dreckschleuder, Verleumder

muff diving
A crude term for performing cunnilingus.
Cunnilingus praktizieren; Perlentauchen

a mug
Someone who is easily fooled, especially when it comes to money.
Naiver Trottel, der sich insbesondere bei Geldangelegenheiten leicht übers Ohr hauen lässt

a mummy's boy
A crybaby, an effeminate male.
Muttersöhnchen

a muppet
Not one of those loveable Sesame Street characters, but a term to describe someone who is useless or foolish.
Depp (hat nichts mit der "Sesamstraße" zu tun)

N is for …
wie …

naff
Useless, kitschy.
Bescheuert, geschmacklos

"Naff off!"
"Get lost!"
"Hau ab!"

namby-pamby
Effeminate, girly.
Verweichlicht

a nancy boy
An effeminate male. Also known as "mummy's boy".
Tunte; Muttersöhnchen

a nasty piece of work
Unpleasant, often violent or aggressive person.
Fieser Typ, Ekelpaket

a ne'er-do-well
A rogue, vagrant or vagabond without means of support; a good-for-nothing louse.
Taugenichts

"Neither use nor ornament!"
A totally useless person.
Zu nichts zu gebrauchen, dumm und hässlich

a nerd (US)
An expression to describe a geek. Usually an unattractive person with an unhealthy interest in things like computers, technology or guns.
Fachidiot; unattraktive Person, die sich für Dinge wie Computer, Technologie oder Waffen interessiert

a nincompoop
An extremely old term for a fool.
Einfaltspinsel (veraltet)

a ninny
A fool, a person who does not really know what is going on.
Dummkopf, Dussel

a nitpicker
A pedant. A person who goes into every tiny detail, several times!
Erbsenzähler, Korinthenkacker

"No shit?" (US)
Nice expression which means "Really?"
"Echt?", "Ohne Scheiß?"

nookie
A frivolous word for sex.
Sex (vulgär)

a nosy cow
An extremely curious female.
Neugierige Kuh, Schnüfflerin

a nosy parker

Someone who pokes his or her nose into everyone else's business.
Schnüffler, der seine Nase in anderer Leute Angelegenheiten steckt

"Not a full carrot!"

A wonderful British expression to describe someone who is not all there, someone who may be lacking in the brain cell department.
Nicht alle Tassen im Schrank haben

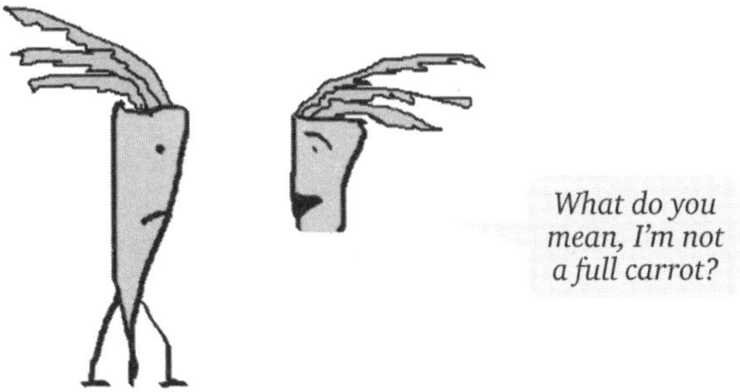

a **numpty**

An inoffensive way of calling someone an idiot.
Trottel

nuts

Crazy; testicles.
Verrückt; Eier (Hoden)

a **nutter** (or **nutcase**)

A crazy person.
Irrer

O is for … wie …

An **odd duck/bird**

A slightly strange, unfathomable person.
Ein seltsamer Vogel

an **oddball**

A strange person, a misfit.
Eigenbrötler, Exzentriker

(to) be **off one's rocker**
Crazy.
Nicht mehr alle Tassen im Schrank haben

(to) be **off one's trolley**
Crazy.
Nicht mehr ganz dicht sein

the **office/town bike**
An unkind reference to a local girl/woman of easy virtue, on whom everybody has had a ride.
Billiges Flittchen; gemeine Umschreibung für eine Frau, die schon mit jedem (im Büro/im Ort) was hatte

an **oik**
Crude, uneducated person.
Proll

an **old biddy/old bag/old hag**
An old woman.
Alte Schachtel

an **old fogey/old goat**
A grumpy old person.
Alter Knacker, alte Ziege

on another planet
Not in touch with reality.
Hinterm Mond leben

(to) be **on the game**
Working as a prostitute.
Auf den Strich gehen

on the job
Having sex.
Es treiben

on the pull
Going to pubs or clubs and looking for a man/woman.
Männer/Frauen aufreißen (in Kneipen, Clubs etc.)

"On yer bike!"
"Get lost!"
"Verzieh' dich!"

(to) be one can short of a six pack.

Slightly stupid.

Nicht ganz helle sein

"(He couldn't) organize a piss-up in a brewery!"

Describing total incompetence.

Nicht bis drei zählen können, völlig inkompetent; "Der könnte nicht mal ein Besäufnis in der Brauerei organisieren!"

OTT

Short for "over the top", overexaggerated.

Übertrieben, zu viel des Guten

over the hill

Past your prime.

Die besten Jahre sind vorbei

P is for …
wie …

a pain in the arse
A lovely expression describing someone who is annoying.
Nervensäge

pampered
Spoilt.
Verzogen, verhätschelt

a **pansy**
A mummy's boy.
Muttersöhnchen, Weichei

pants
Rubbish, crap.
Mist

a **parasite**
Someone who lives off someone else. (Often used to describe students.)
Schmarotzer (v. a. Studenten)

a **party pooper**
A miserable person who spoils all the fun.
Spaßbremse

(to) be **past it**
Too old, unable to do the things you used to do.
Der Zug ist abgefahren

a **pavement pizza**
A graphic term for vomit.
Bildliche Beschreibung für Erbrochenes auf dem Gehweg

pea-brain
Of very low intelligence.
Erbsenhirn

a **pen pusher**
A mocking term for someone who works in an office.
Schreibtischhengst, Sesselfurzer

a **pervert** (also a **perv**)
A sexual fiend.
Perversling

pervy
Perverted.
Pervers

petty (or **petty-minded**)
Narrow-minded, mean or lacking generosity, especially in trifling matters.
Kleinkariert, engstirnig

a **pig**
A swine. A dirty person. Also a person who has behaved badly.
Schwein

a **pillock**
Old-fashioned word to describe an idiot.
Idiot (veraltet)

a **pinhead**
An idiot.
Dummkopf

piss
Urine.
Pisse, Urin

(to) take a piss (also a leak, a slash, a Jimmy Riddle, a piddle, to drain the main vain)
(To) urinate.
Pinkeln, strullern, pissen

(to) **take the piss/the mickey** out of sb.
(To) make fun of someone.
Sich über jemanden lustig machen, jemanden verarschen

on the piss (also **on a bender, on the razzle, painting the town red, on the town**)
Drinking (alcohol) excessively.
Sich maßlos betrinken, (be)saufen

a **piss artist** (or **pisshead**)
Someone, usually a man, who drinks alcohol to excess.
Säufer, Suffkopf

"Piss off!"
A rather nasty and direct way of telling someone that their presence is no longer required.
"Verpiss dich!"

pissed (also **as pissed as a fart, as pissed as a newt, bladdered, paralytic, plastered, legless, blind drunk, Brahms & Liszt**)
Extremely drunk.
Total besoffen (UK); in den USA bedeutet "pissed" jedoch "stinksauer"

pissed off
Depressed, annoyed, fed up.
Angepisst, genervt, schlecht drauf

"What a pisser!"
An expression of extreme disappointment.
"So eine Scheiße!"

pissing around
Being foolish.
Herumalbern

"It's pissing (it) down."
A crude term for "it's raining".
"Es pisst/schifft."

piss-poor
Sub-standard, very bad.
Abgebrannt (arm); erbärmlich, hundsmiserabel

a **pisstaker**
The person who's "taking the piss".
Jemand, der sich über andere lustig macht

a **piss-up**
A heavy drinking session.
Saufgelage, Besäufnis

a **pleb**
Lowlife citizen. Commoner. Scum.
Proll

plonk
A colloquial term for wine.
Plörre (billiger Wein)

a **plonker**
An idiot.
Knallkopf, Trottel

po-faced
Miserable.
Mürrisch, sauertöpfisch

a **ponce**
Originally this word was used to describe a pimp (someone who lives off the immoral earnings of prostitutes). Nowadays it refers to someone who dresses or behaves in an affected way or someone who is rather effeminate: "He is a bit poncey!"
Ursprünglich Zuhälter, heute auch Tunte

a **porker**
A fat person. Referring to the type of pigs that are specially bred and fattened up for market.
Fettsack

a **poser**
A show-off, someone who likes to be the centre of attention.
Angeber, Poser

potty
Crazy.
Plemplem, verrückt

poxy
Awful, terrible.
Beschissen, blöd

a **prannock**
An old-fashioned term for an idiot.
Idiot (veraltet)

a **prat**
A snide way of referring to someone who you think is an idiot.
Trottel

a **prick**
Another male appendage colloquialism used to describe someone, usually a man, who you do not think highly of.
Schwanz; Scheißkerl, Arschloch

a **pricktease(r)**
An extremely depreciative term describing a woman who flaunts herself in front of men, while at the same time having no intention of taking the relationship further.
Eine Frau, die Männer scharfmacht und dann abblitzen lässt

prim and proper
Prudish.
Etepetete

a **prima donna**
Someone who likes to act as if they are the star attraction wherever they go.
Primadonna; jemand, der gerne im Mittelpunkt steht

private parts or **privates**
Genitalia.
Geschlechtsteile

a pro
A prostitute.
Nutte

a proper little madam
A very young, assertive girl who knows what she wants and how to get it.
Prinzesschen; ein kleines Mädchen, das genau weiß, was es will und wie man es bekommt

a prude
Someone who doesn't do things that are fun, such as drinking and partying.
Langweiler, Spießer

a psycho
Totally crazy. (Short for psychopath.)
Psychopath

a pudding
A bit of an idiot. Sometimes used as a term of endearment: "You great big pudding!"
Dummerchen, auch als Kosename

puddled
Crazy or confused.
Verrückt, verwirrt

a puff or **poofter (also woofter and nufter)**
A scathing term to describe someone who might or might not be homosexual.
Tunte

pug-ugly (also pig-ugly, as ugly as sin)
Very ugly person.
Extrem hässlich

(to) puke (also to **chuck up**, to **spew one's guts up**, to **be as sick as a dog**, to **barf**, to **chunder**)
Colloquial terms for vomiting (being sick).
Kotzen, reihern

"As pure as the driven snow."
Virginal, whiter than white. Frequently used in a sarcastic way to describe a hypocrite.
Jungfräulich, so unschuldig wie ein Engel; meistens ironisch gebraucht

pushy
Brash, persistent.
Aufdringlich, dreist

pussy
A colloquial term for the vagina.
Muschi

"Put that in your pipe and smoke it!"
An expression of vindication or triumph.
"So ist es, ob es dir passt oder nicht!"

Q is for … / wie …

a queen or an **old queen**

An extremely effeminate, older male. Often very feminine or camp in appearance and behaviour.

Ein in seinem Auftreten und Verhalten sehr auffälliger älterer Schwuler

a queer; queer

One of the very first expressions used to describe a homosexual male.

Schwuler; schwul. Einer der allerersten Ausdrücke für männliche Homosexuelle

a quickie

Quick sex.

Quickie, schneller Sex

R is for … / wie …

a radish

A boring person.

Langweiler

randy

Sexually excited. Often used to describe insatiable sexual animals both male and female.

Geil

a (little) rascal

A badly behaved young child.

Frechdachs, Früchtchen

a rat

Also known as "love rat". A man who treats women abominably.

Miese Ratte, Mistkerl; ein Mann, der Frauen unmöglich behandelt

rat-arsed or **rat-faced**
Extremely drunk.
Sternhagelvoll

a **raving loony** or **lunatic**
A loud, unstable, rambling individual.
Ein/e komplett Gestörte/r

a **redneck** (US)
The term is chiefly used for a poor, rural white person of the Southern United States, also known as "hillbilly".
Hinterwäldler, Prolet (v. a. Weiße in den Südstaaten der USA)

a **rent boy**
A young, male prostitute.
Stricher

riff-raff (also **rabble**)
A snobbish description of lower-class people, but often used in a light-hearted way. (Example: "Don't talk to that riff-raff/rabble, my dear.")
Gesindel, Gesocks, Pöbel

a **rip-off merchant**
A businessman or individual renowned for cheating people (i.e. car salesmen, etc.)
Abzocker, Halsabschneider (Geschäftsmann, z. B. Autohändler, der einen übers Ohr hauen will)

(to) **roger**
To fuck someone.
Jemanden nageln

round the twist/bend
Crazy.
Einen an der Waffel haben, einen Klaps haben

a **rubbernecker; rubbernecking**
A nosy person. Someone who stretches their neck to get a better look, especially at car crash scenes.
Gaffer; gaffen

rude
Discourteous or impolite.
Unhöflich, unanständig

a **ruffian**
A troublemaker, a bad boy.
Raufbold, Rüpel

a rum bugger
A person of questionable character.
Komischer Kauz

rumpy pumpy
A coy term for having sex.
Neckische Umschreibung für Sex

S is for … / wie …

a saddo
A pathetic person.
Armseliger Idiot

sarky
Short for "sarcastic".
Sarkastisch

Sassenach (Scottish)
What the Scots call those swine south of the border.
Schottisches Schimpfwort für Engländer

a scab
A traitor. Usually a strikebreaker.
Verräter, vor allem Streikbrecher

a scarlet woman
A sexually promiscuous woman, especially one guilty of committing adultery.
Liederliches Frauenzimmer, Ehebrecherin (veraltet)

scatty
Absent-minded and disorganized.
Schusselig

a schmuck
A horrible person.
Arschloch, Fiesling

a scoundrel
A thoroughly despicable person, a liar and a cheat.
Halunke, Kanaille

a screw; screwing
A colloquial term for having sex. (A "screw" could also be a prison officer.)
Fick (auch: Gefängniswärter); vögeln

"(He/she's got) a **screw loose!**"
Not completely sane.
"Er/sie hat eine Schraube locker!"

"Screw you!"
"Go to hell!"
"Leck mich am Arsch!"

a **scrounger**
A person who is always asking for things for free (i.e. money, food, drinks, etc.).
Schnorrer

a **scrubber**
A woman of loose moral standards, seen as easy prey by both men and women.
Flittchen

a **scruff; scruffy**
Untidy, unkempt, dirty.
Ungepflegte Person; schlampig, schmuddelig

scum (or a **scumbag**)
Dishonest and/or despicable person.
Abschaum, Drecksack

seedy
A dirty, rundown horrible place. (Example: "I went to a really seedy nightclub last night.")
Zwielichtig, heruntergekommen

"(Someone's had) a **sense of humour by-pass operation**."
This describes a person with absolutely no sense of humour whatsoever.
Absolut keinen Humor haben

a **septic**
Cockney rhyming slang: "septic tank" – "Yank", meaning an American.
Ami

a **serial quitter**
Someone who moves quickly from one job to another.
Versager, der ständig den Job wechselt

shagged out

Looking/feeling bedraggled or very tired. This could also apply to the way someone looks/feels after extensive shagging.
Fix und fertig, auch im Sinne von "durchgevögelt"

shagging

A coarse term for having sex.
Pimpern, vögeln

"Shaking like a shitting dog."

Someone of a very nervous disposition.
Sich vor Aufregung in die Hose machen

a **sheepshagger**

A nasty expression that implies someone has a tendency to have sex with sheep. Often used in reference to country folk, or people deemed as uneducated, of low intelligence or simple.
Schafsficker; häufig in Bezug auf "Landeier" oder vermeintlich ungebildete, dumme Menschen verwendet

a **shirker**

"(To) shirk" means to avoid. A shirker is someone who avoids any form of hard work.
Drückeberger

a **shirtlifter**

An unpleasant term for a male homosexual.
Schwuler (abwertend)

shit

Universally-known swearword.
Scheiße; universell einsetzbares Schimpfwort

a (little) **shit**

An expression that describes someone as the lowest form of crap. Usually reserved for instances of hurt, anguish or back-stabbing: "He did what? The little shit!"
Scheißkerl; "Dieses (kleine) Stück Scheiße!"

"Eat shit!"

A gloating, gleeful retort to a rival who has been proven wrong.
Schadenfrohe Antwort gegenüber jemandem, der falsch gelegen hat

"I couldn't **give a shit/a fuck!"**

Stronger versions of "I couldn't give a toss!" meaning "I couldn't care less!"
"Das geht mir am Arsch vorbei!"

"He wouldn't give you the steam off his shit!"

A miser.

Geizhals, Geizkragen

"Shit for brains."

A great put-down for a stupid rival or someone you do not like.

"Du hast nur Scheiße im Hirn."

"Shit happens."

The English version of the French "C'est la vie".

"Dumm gelaufen!", "So ist das Leben!"

"The shit has hit the fan!"

A superb expression to describe the consequences of someone's action.

"Jetzt ist die Kacke am Dampfen!"

"Shite!"

A rougher version of "shit!"

Etwas härtere Version von "shit"

a **shitehawk**

A horrible, despicable person.

Scheißkerl

shit-faced

Incredibly drunk.

Stockbesoffen

a **shithead** or **shitface**

A detestable person.

Scheißkerl

the **shits** (also the **squirts**, the **runs** and **shitting through the eye of a needle**)

Diarrhea.

Dünnschiss

a **shitshifter**

A rather nasty term for a male homosexual.

Schwuchtel

shitting bricks (also **shit scared**, **scared shitless** and **shitting yourself**)

Extremely afraid.

Sich vor Angst in die Hose scheißen, Schiss haben

shitty

Terrible.

Beschissen

"Short arms and deep pockets."

Someone who doesn't like to pay for anything, especially a round of drinks.

Beschreibt einen Geizhals, der sich insbesondere drückt, eine Runde Drinks auszugeben

a **short-arse**

A short person.

Winzling, Zwerg

"Shove off!"

Go away.

"Schieb ab!"

"Shove it/stick it up your arse!"
Wonderfully direct retort leaving no room for misunderstandings.
"Das kannst du dir in den Arsch schieben!"

"Shove it where the sun doesn't shine!"
Politer version of the above.
"Das kannst du dir da hin stecken, wo die Sonne nicht scheint!"

a **shower**
A group of people, for example the England football team, who have performed badly.
Eine Gruppe Versager, z. B. eine Fußballmannschaft

"Shut your cake hole!" (Also **"Shut your gob!"**)
Alternative versions of "shut up!"
"Halt die Fresse!"

a **sicko**
A pervert. A nasty, often masochistic person.
Perversling, Geistesgestörter

a **sissy**
A boy who is weak or who likes things that girls usually like and cries easily.
Weichei, Heulsuse

a **skinflint**
A miser.
Knauser, Geizkragen

a **skiver; (to) skive off**
A lazy person; to deliberately avoid working.
Drückeberger; blaumachen

a **slag**
A term that many women use to describe other women they see as free and easy when it comes to sex.
Schlampe (Schimpfwort unter Frauen)

slap and tickle
A funny term for sex. "Fancy a bit of slap and tickle?"
Humorvoller Begriff für Sex

a **slaphead**
A bald person.
Glatzkopf

a **slapper**
A loose woman, often seen as unattractive, yet sexually active.
Schlampe, unattraktive promiskuitive Frau

having a **slash**
A course term for having a pee.
Schiffen, strullern

a **sleazebag**
A person of low moral standards. Often used to describe politicians who have been caught with their trousers down or their noses in the financial trough.
Schmieriger Typ (oft Politiker, die in Sexaffären oder krumme Geschäfte verwickelt sind)

a **slimeball/a slimy bastard**
Unprincipled in pursuit of favours or advancement. Also known as a "suck-up".
Schleimer, Arschkriecher

"Sling your hook!"
A great way of telling someone to go away.
"Mach die Fliege!"

a **Sloane Ranger (sometimes shortened to "Sloane")**
A stereotype of young, middle-class people who share distinctive and common lifestyle traits. The term is a pun of Sloane Square, a location in Chelsea, London, known for the wealth of residents and the television western character "the Lone Ranger".
Junger Angehöriger der gehobenen Mittelschicht Londons

a **slob**
Lazy, invariably overweight and untidy. "Couch potato" is the more modern term.
Faulenzer, Gammler

sloshed
Drunk.
Besoffen

a **slouch**
A lazy or slovenly person.
Gammler, Niete

(to) be **slow on the uptake**
Simple.
Eine lange Leitung haben

a slut
An extremely sexually active female who is not too choosy about her sexual partners.
Schlampe, die jeden nimmt

a smack in the kisser
"To smack" means to punch or slap, "kisser" is the colloquial term for the mouth. Put the two together and you get a punch in the mouth.
Ein Schlag in die Fresse

a smart arse (also a smart Alec)
A know-all – inevitably proven right.
Besserwisser, Klugscheißer

a smug bastard
An extremely self-satisfied, over-confident person who is very pleased with him-/herself.
Selbstzufriedenes Arschloch

smutty
Dirty, pornographic.
Schmutzig, versaut

a snake
An untrustworthy person.
Hinterhältige Schlange

a snapper
A person who loses their temper quickly.
Choleriker

a snitch; (to) snitch
Someone who reveals a secret, a big mouth.
Petze; petzen

a snob; snobby
Aloof, arrogant and invariably unfriendly. "Toffee-nosed" and "stuck up" also apply here.
Snob; snobistisch

a snotty-nosed cow
A posh, arrogant, often aloof woman.
Eingebildete Gans

a social leper
An outsider, a social outcast.
Sozialer Außenseiter

a sod
A little rascal. Often used in a friendly way: “Oh, you little sod!”
Drecksack; oft in neckisch-freundlichem Ton gebraucht: “Du kleiner Drecksack!”

“Sod all!”
Nothing.
“Rein gar nichts!”

“Sod it!”
“To hell with it!”
“Verdammter Mist!”

“Sod off!”
Somewhere between “bugger off” and “piss off”.
“Zieh Leine!”

“Sod/fuck this for a game of soldiers!”
An expression of disquiet, when you find yourself doing something you really don’t want to do or you are totally fed up with doing something.
“Darauf habe ich keinen Bock (mehr)!”

“Sod you!”
Mild form of “fuck you!”
“Leck mich am Arsch!”

“Sodding hell!”
Mild form of “fucking hell!”
Weniger vulgäre Variante von “fucking hell!”

soft in the head
Stupid, foolish.
Weich in der Birne

a soft touch
Someone who is seen as easy to persuade to help or part with money.
Leichte Beute

soppy
Overly sentimental.
Gefühlsduselig, schnulzig

a sour-faced puss
An extremely miserable person.
Griesgram, Miesepeter

a spade
A politically incorrect word for a black person.
Neger (politisch unkorrekt)

a spastic
A politically incorrect term for a person who is not very mobile or agile.
Spasti (ebenfalls politisch unkorrekt)

Specky Four-Eyes
An age-old children's taunt for someone wearing glasses.
Brillenschlange (Kindersprache)

(going to) spend a penny (also seeing a man about a dog)
A polite way of telling someone you are going to the toilet.
Für kleine Mädchen/Jungs gehen, aufs Klo gehen

spineless
Cowardly. Without backbone.
Rückgratlos, feige

spitting blood/feathers
Extremely angry.
Vor Wut platzen

a spoilt brat
A young, pampered child. More often than not out of control and unruly.
Verzogenes Balg

a sponger; (to) sponge
To live off other people or their money.
Schmarotzer; schnorren

Spotty Muldoon
Old-fashioned children's taunt for a child with spots on their face.
Pickelgesicht (Kindersprache)

spunk
Colloquial word for semen (can also mean courage).
Sperma; aber auch Mumm, Mut

stark (bollock) naked or **starkers**
Without clothes.
Splitterfasernackt

"Sticks and stones ..."
The full version is "Sticks and stones may break my bones, but names will never hurt me." A great retort to someone who is trying to wind you up or annoy you with criticism or name-calling.
"Hier rein und da raus!" (als Erwiderung auf Beleidigungen etc.)

a **stick-in-the-mud**
A person who avoids new activities, ideas or attitudes.
Muffel, Langweiler, der nichts Neues ausprobiert

a **stiffy**
A sexually erect penis.
Ständer, Latte

a **stinker**
A horrible person.
Stinker, Ekel

stinking rich
Incredibly wealthy.
Stinkreich

a **stirrer** or **shit-stirrer**
Someone who likes to cause trouble amongst other people, often by relating things said in confidence.
Aufhetzer, Giftspritze

stroppy or **in a strop**
Moody, offhand.
Patzig, eingeschnappt

a **strumpet**
A slut, a loose woman.
Dirne, Flittchen

"As stubborn as a mule!"
To be very determined not to change your decision or opinion about something, even if you are wrong.
"Stur wie ein Esel!"

Sometimes you're as stubborn as a human!

stuck-up
Snobbish.
Hochnäsig

"Get stuffed!"
Mild form of "fuck off!"
"Leck mich doch!"

stuffy (also **staid**)
A very conservative person. Boring. Often without humour.
Spießig, bieder

"He/she looks like they've **swallowed a wasp!**"
Dour-faced.
Ein Gesicht machen wie drei Tage Regenwetter

"You suck!" (US)
An excellent American expression which basically means "You are a piece of crap, you can't do anything right." And all said in two words. Great!
"Ich find dich zum Kotzen, du bekommst nichts auf die Reihe!" Herrlicher amerikanischer Ausdruck, der mit zwei Worten alles Wichtige sagt!

a **sucker**
Someone who is easily taken in or fooled.
Trottel, Einfaltspinsel

"He/she looks like they've been **sucking on a lemon**."
Another description for a sour-faced puss!
Ein mürrisches/sauertöpfisches Gesicht machen

a **suck-up**
A sycophant.
Arschkriecher, Schleimscheißer

a **sugar daddy**
A rich, older man who is sought by "gold diggers" or "moneygrabbers".
Reicher älterer Mann, der eine junge Frau aushält

a **suphead**
"(To) sup" is a colloquial word meaning "(to) drink". A "suphead" drinks a lot.
Schluckspecht

sweet Fanny Adams
Nothing. Example: "What did you get out of it? Sweet Fanny Adams!" (from "sweet FA" – "fuck all".)
Rein gar nichts; Euphemismus für "fuck all"

a **swine**
A pig, a nasty man.
Schwein

T is for … wie …

"Take a hike!"
"Go away!"
"Mach die Fliege!"

"Takes one to know one!"
This is an excellent retort with which you can turn the tables on someone who is insulting you: "You're a loudmouth!" – "Takes one to know one!"
"Das sagt der/die Richtige!" (Entgegnung auf eine Beleidigung)

(to) **talk the hind legs off a donkey**
To never stop talking. A chatterbox.
Jemandem ein Ohr abkauen

a **tart**
A prostitute or a woman who gives sex away freely.
Nutte, Schlampe

"You tart!"
A way of telling someone you think they are acting like a little girl.
Ausdruck, um jemandem zu sagen, dass er sich wie ein kleines Mädchen benimmt.

teacher's pet
The teacher's favourite pupil. Usually academically gifted and well-behaved.
Streber, Lehrerliebling

a tearaway
An uncontrollable young child.
Rabauke

a tell-tale
Children's expression to describe someone who reveals secrets.
Petze (Kindersprache)

"That makes two of us!"
A great way of countering criticism from someone else. Example: "You're stupid!"– "That makes two of us!"
"Da sind wir schon zu zweit!" (Entgegnung auf eine Beleidigung)

"That takes the biscuit!"
An expression of complete disgust at another's actions.
"Das schlägt dem Fass den Boden aus!"

"There's one born every minute!"
An expression used when somebody behaves very gullibly.
"Die Dummen sterben nicht aus."

thick; as thick as pig shit
Extremely stupid.
Dumm; dumm wie Scheiße

as thick as two short planks
A milder version of the above.
Strohdumm, dumm wie Bohnenstroh

a thingy
A childish name for a penis.
Pillermann, Dingsda (Penis)

a thug (also a "Neanderthal")
A vicious, violent, often uneducated male.
Schlägertyp, Rowdy

thunder thighs
An unkind description of a woman with large thighs.
Frau mit dicken Oberschenkeln

a tightarse (also a **scrooge**); **tight** (also **tight-fisted, as tight as a duck's arse, so tight he squeaks when he walks**)

Miserly, loath to part with money. Bearing a striking resemblance to Ebenezer Scrooge.

Geizhals; knauserig (wie man sich Ebenezer Scrooge aus Dickens' Weihnachtserzählung vorstellt)

a tit

Vulgar word for a woman's breast, also used to describe a stupid person. "He's a right tit!"

Titte; auch im Sinne von "dumme Sau" verwendet

"You get on my tits!"

You are extremely annoying!

"Du gehst mir auf den Sack!"

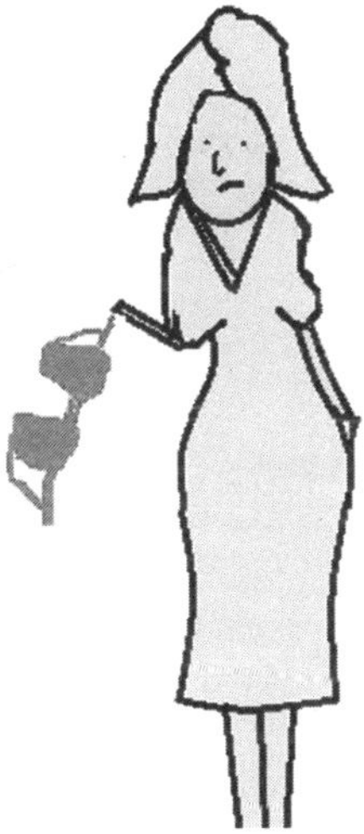

a tithead

A variation of "tit".

Dummkopf

todger

Inoffensive name for a penis.

Schwanz, Penis

a toerag

Another word for "scumbag".

Mistkerl, Drecksack

a toff

A rich, snobbish person, usually belonging to the upper classes or royalty.

Reicher Schnösel, feiner Pinkel

toffee-nosed
Snobbish.
Hochnäsig, arrogant

Tommies
German slang for English soldiers.
Britische Soldaten (v. a. seit dem Ersten Weltkrieg weit verbreitete Bezeichnung in Deutschland. Der Begriff geht zurück auf den Soldaten Thomas Atkins, dessen Name seit dem 19. Jh. in den Musterformularen der britischen Armee verwendet wurde.)

a **tool**
Yet another example of a euphemism for the male appendage used to call someone a fool.
Schwanz, Ding (Penis), auch im Sinne von "Idiot" verwendet

"Tosh!"
Rubbish! Nonsense!
"Quatsch!"

"I couldn't give a **toss!"**
A great retort meaning "I couldn't care less!"
"Das geht mir am Arsch vorbei!"

a **tosser** or a **tosspot**
"(To) toss" is a colloquialism for masturbation. A "tosser" is therefore a "wanker".
Wichser

totty
A male, macho term for available women. (Example: "Wow! Look at all the totty in here!")
Machobegriff für Frauen, die zu haben sind; Weiber, Schnecken

"Tough shit!"
A retort meaning "I don't care!"
"Dumm gelaufen!" (schadenfroh)

"Tough titty!"
A sarcastic way of saying "hard luck!"
"Pech gehabt!" (sarkastisch)

a **toy boy**
An older woman's much younger boyfriend.
Deutlich jüngerer Sexgespiele einer älteren Frau

trailer trash (US)
Lower-class, poorly educated people living on trailer parks.
Amerikanische Unterschicht, die in Wohnwagenkolonien lebt

a **tramp**
Offensive description of a loose woman who has sex freely (also a homeless man).
Schlampe; Obdachloser

a **trollop**
A wanton female of easy virtue.
Flittchen

a **turd**
Literally a piece of shit, which quite nicely sums up this insult.
Stück Scheiße

a **turncoat**
A backstabber. Someone who changes allegiance without warning.
Wendehals, Verräter

twaddle
Nonsense. For example: "You are talking a load of twaddle!"
Quatsch, Unsinn

a **twerp**
Old-fashioned word for idiot.
Blödmann, Knalltüte (veraltet)

a **twit**
A foolishly annoying person.
Depp

two-faced
Insincere, hypocritical, dishonest, deceitful.
Doppelzüngig, hinterhältig, heuchlerisch

U is for ... wie ...

up the duff (also up the spout and up the stick)

Colloquial terms for a woman who is pregnant.

Schwanger

(to) drive somebody up the wall

(To) drive somebody crazy.

Jemanden in den Wahnsinn treiben

"Up yours!" (Also "Swivel on that!")

A slightly politer form of "fuck you!"

"Du kannst mich mal!"

uptight

Unable to relax and just chill. Tense.

Verklemmt, überspannt

V is for ... wie ...

verbal diarrhea

A wonderful expression describing what comes out of the mouth of someone who is talking "bullshit".

Scheiße labern

a **villain**

A criminal or wicked person.

Schurke, Gauner, Schuft, Verbrecher

W is for … wie …

a **wacko; wacky**

A person regarded as eccentric or irrational.

Spinner; bekloppt, schrullig

a **wally**

An idiot.

Trottel

a **waste of space**

A useless person.

Ein durch und durch nutzloser Mensch, die reinste Platzverschwendung

a **wazzock**

An old-fashioned, inoffensive word meaning "fool".

Dummkopf (veraltet)

"We are not amused!"

A famous quote by Queen Victoria stating her displeasure.

"Wir sind nicht erfreut!" (berühmtes Zitat von Queen Victoria)

a **weasel**

A horrible, underhanded person.

Betrüger, hinterhältige Person

a **weed; weedy**

A weak, ineffectual man.

Hänfling, Schwächling; schmächtig

a **weirdo; weird**

A person regarded as being very strange or eccentric. Potentially dangerous person.

Schräger Vogel, komischer Kauz; irre, seltsam

wet behind the ears

Naïve.

Grün hinter den Ohren, unerfahren, naiv

a **wet blanket**

A person who tends to spoil other people's enjoyment through negativity or general lack of enthusiasm.

Spielverderber, Spaßbremse

a **wet fish**

A boring person.

Langweiler

"What a load of …"

Many words can be inserted here: "… crap/bullshit/bollocks/ rubbish!" It all means the same, you think someone is talking crap.

"Was für ein Haufen Scheiße/Mist/Unsinn/Quatsch!"

"What the fuck?"

An expression of complete surprise. This expression can be used on its own, or as the opening to a sentence. For example: "What the fuck are you doing?"

Ausdruck totaler Überraschung, kann alleine stehen oder als Einleitung: "Was zur Hölle/zum Henker/zum Teufel (machst du da)?"

"Which planet do you live on?"

A nice expression to use on someone who doesn't want to face up to reality.

"Auf welchem Planeten lebst du denn?!"

a **whiner**

"Whining" is the same as "whinging". A whiner usually complains in a highly irritating voice.

Jammerlappen

a **whinger**

"(To) whinge" means to complain or moan. A "whinger" does both.

Nörgler

white trash (US)

Poor, uneducated white people.

Abschaum, arme und ungebildete weiße Unterschicht der USA

"Who rattled your cage?"
Great expression that means "this has nothing to do with you."
"Wer hat dich gefragt?"

"Why don't you (just) …"
This is a brilliant prefix for all kinds of insults. (Examples: "Why don't you … bugger off/shove it up your arse/piss off!")
Gute Einleitung für etliche Beleidigungen, z. B.: "Warum verpisst du dich nicht einfach?!"

willy
Children's term for penis.
Pimmel, Schniedelwutz

a **wimp**
"As soft as shite" as the saying goes. This can refer to the physical as well as the mental weakness of someone.
Weichei, Schlappschwanz

a **windbag**
Full of hot air. Usually takes a long time to say very little.
Dummschwätzer, Labertasche

a **wino**
A drunk.
Trinker

"With friends like you, who needs enemies?"
Light-hearted banter used amongst friends.
"Wer solche Freunde hat, braucht keine Feinde mehr!" (scherzhaft unter Freunden)

witless
Clueless, rather stupid.
Dumm, einfältig

a **wobblebottom**
A person with so much fat around their posterior that it wobbles when they move, on the rare occasions such people *do* actually move.
Wabbelarsch, Fettsack

a **woman of easy virtue**
A female who, it is assumed, is easy to get into bed.
Leichtes Mädchen

a womaniser

A philanderer, a man who likes many women and has short sexual relationships with them.

Schürzenjäger, Frauenheld

a working girl

A euphemism for a prostitute.

Prostituierte

a worm

A person with little moral fibre, who will wriggle and squirm their way out of a tricky situation.

Wurm, Schleimer; jemand mit geringen moralischen Maßstäben

"Wouldn't touch it with a bargepole!"

Used for situations that you would do your best to avoid at all costs.

"Das würde ich nicht mal mit der Kneifzange anfassen!"

a wuss

A person regarded as weak or timid and especially as unmanly.

Waschlappen, Weichei

X is for ... X-rated Nicht jugendfrei!

Warning: All the words in this section are extremely offensive and using them will almost certainly cause offence. Use with care.

Warnung: Die folgenden Wörter sollten nur mit äußerster Vorsicht verwendet werden, da sie für mächtig Ärger sorgen können!

a bitch

A horrible term to describe a woman.

Nutte, Schlampe

a cocksucker (US)

An extremely offensive American insult that could lead to violence if used in the wrong company.

Schwanzlutscher; dieses Wort sollte man besser nicht in schlechter Gesellschaft gebrauchen

a cunt

Another vulgar word for the vagina. Possibly the worst insult you can use against someone in the UK.

Fotze; wahrscheinlich das schlimmste Schimpfwort in Großbritannien

a minge
A vulgar term for the vagina.
Möse

a motherfucker (US)
An extremely vulgar and insulting term.
Mutterficker

a son of a bitch
An awful insult to direct at someone personally. Can be used generally as an expression of frustration if something has gone wrong: "Son of a bitch!"
Hurensohn; auch "Verdammte Scheiße!"

a twat
Originally a vulgar term for the female vagina, now also used to describe somebody who you dislike intensely. This word is even more offensive than "bastard".
Fotze; heutzutage auch im Sinne von "Arschloch" verwendet

a wanker
Literally means "masturbator".
Wichser

a whore
An extremely derogatory term for a woman.
Nutte, Hure

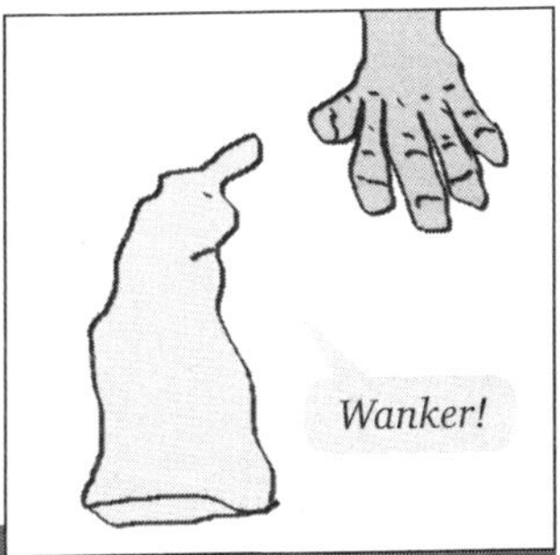

Y is for … / wie …

a yob or a yobbo
A hooligan.
Rowdy, Rüpel, Halbstarker

a (country) yokel
A simple, poorly-educated person from the country.
Bauerntrampel

"You can dish it out, but you can't take it!"
This is a retort for someone who is quite happy to "dish out" their own insults, but who takes great offense when you criticise them.
"Du kannst nur austeilen, aber nicht einstecken!"

"You know what you can do!"
This basically means "kiss my arse!"
"Du kannst mich mal!"

"You look like death warmed up!"
More an observation than an insult. Usually reserved for people who have had a very late night.
"Du siehst aus wie der Tod persönlich!" (Mehr eine Feststellung als eine Beleidigung, z. B. nach einer durchzechten Nacht)

"You need your head examined!"
"You must be crazy!"
"Du bist doch total bekloppt!"

"You wish!"
Great retort to someone who is rather presumptuous.
"Das hättest du wohl gerne!"

a yuppie
A young, upwardly mobile, arrogant individual. Usually used to describe up-and-coming businessmen or politicians.
Yuppie (steht für "young urban professional"), karrierebewusster junger Großstadtmensch

Z is for … wie …

zitface
"A zit" is a spot. "Zitface" refers to someone whose face is covered in spots.
Pickelfresse

zombie
Literally "zombies" are the slow-moving living dead. This expression is usually made about someone who has had a heavy night and is moving around very slowly – like a zombie.
Zombie, Schnapsleiche

Appendix 1 – Gestures
Anhang 1 – Gesten

"Fuck off!"
Also known as "the two fingered salute".
"Fick dich!"

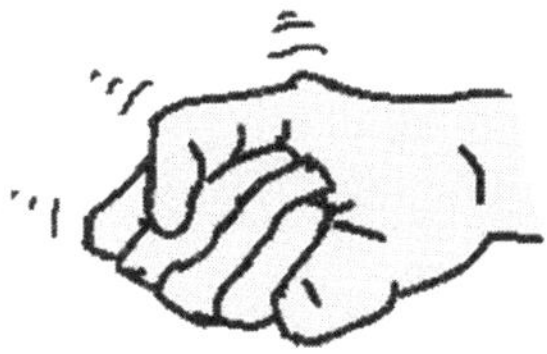

Wanker
Wichser

Loser
Hand must be held in front of forehead.
Versager

"Up yours!"
"Swivel on that!"
"Fick dich!"

Appendix 2 – Regional swearwords
Anhang 2 – Regionale Schimpfwörter

Manchester
(Mancunian)

"Bobbins!"
Not very good.
Mist

a **cadger**
Someone who is always asking for things.
Schnorrer

daft 'apeth
A harmless term for a fool.
Dummkopf

"Get off and milk it!"
Greeting to a cyclist.
Scherzhafter Gruß an Fahrradfahrer

"He couldn't stop a pig in a ginnel."
Describes someone who has bandy (bent) legs.
Beschreibung für jemanden mit O-Beinen: "Der könnte nicht mal in einer engen Gasse ein Schwein aufhalten!"

"Mingin'!"
Unpleasant.
Eklig

Newcastle
(Geordie)

a **doylem**
Idiot, fool.
Idiot

hacky
Dirty. (Can also mean lazy.)
Schmutzig, faul

micey
Showing signs of madness.
Plemplem

nebby
Nosy, inquisitive.
Neugierig

Yorkshire

nesh
Afraid.
Feige

"There's nowt as queer as folk!"
Expression meaning "there is nothing in life stranger than people".
Etwa: "Es gibt nichts Seltsameres als Menschen."

Liverpool
(Scouse)

a **beaut**
An idiot.
Depp

bevvied up
Drunk.
Besoffen

jarg
Of bad quality.
Schrottig

a **meff**
A smelly, bad-dressed person.
Stinkende, schlecht gekleidete Person

a **soft lad**
A friendly name for a fool.
Dummer Kerl (freundschaftlich)

Birmingham
(Brummie)

a **face as long as Livery Street**
Miserable.
Ein Gesicht wie drei Tage Regenwetter, erbärmlich, jämmerlich

half-soaked
Stupid or slow-witted.
Dumm

noggy
Old-fashioned or outdated.
Altmodisch, von vorgestern

yampy
Daft or mad or losing the plot.
Bescheuert, verrückt, planlos

Appendix 3 – Cockney rhyming slang
Anhang 3 – Cockney Rhyming Slang

A true Cockney is someone born within the sound of Bow Bells. (St Mary-le-Bow Church in Cheapside, London). However the term Cockney is now loosely applied to many born outside this area as long as they have a "Cockney" accent or a Cockney heritage. Rhyming Slang replaces the original word with an expression, the last word of which rhymes with the original word. For example the word "look" rhymes with "butcher's hook". In many cases the rhyming word is omitted – so you won't find too many Londoners having "a butcher's hook", but you might find a few having "a butcher's". The rhyming word is not always omitted so Cockney expressions can vary in their construction, and it is simply a matter of convention which version is used.

Ein echter Cockney ist jemand, der in Hörweite der Glocken der Kirche St. Mary-le-Bow in Cheapside, London, aufgewachsen ist. Heutzutage nennt man auch diejenigen Cockney, die zwar nicht direkt aus der Umgebung stammen, aber zumindest einen Cockney-Akzent haben oder deren familiäre Wurzeln in dieser Gegend sind. "Cockney Rhyming Slang" bedeutet Folgendes: Das Wort, das man ausdrücken will (z. B. "look"), wird durch einen mehrteiligen Ausdruck ersetzt, der sich auf dieses Wort reimt (z. B. "butcher's hook"). Oft (aber nicht zwangsläufig) wird dann nur der erste Teil des Reimbegriffs verwendet. Statt "have a look" sagt der Cockney "have a butcher's". Regeln gibt es keine. Nur Eingeweihte wissen auf Anhieb, was mit folgenden Cockney-Flüchen gemeint ist …

Cockney *Cockney-Reim*	**Meaning** *Man meint*	**How to use it** *Man sagt*
aristotle	bottle (and glass) → arse *Arsch*	"Nice aris!" *"Geiler Arsch!"*
boracic lint (also: brassic)	skint *pleite*	"I'm absolutely brassic until payday." *"Ich bin total pleite bis zum nächsten Gehalt."*
bottle and glass	arse *Arsch*	"He fell on his bottle." *"Er ist auf den Arsch gefallen."*
brown bread	dead *tot*	"He's brown bread." *"Er ist tot."*
Jimmy Riddle	piddle (urinate) *pinkeln*	"I really need a Jimmy." *"Ich muss mal pissen."*
Khyber Pass	arse *Arsch*	"He kicked him up the Khyber." *"Er hat ihm 'nen Arschtritt verpasst."*
cream crackered	knackered (tired/broken) *im Arsch sein*	"I'm cream crackered!" *"Ich bin voll im Arsch!"*
pen and ink	stink *stinken*	"Ugh! That pen and inks!" *"Iiiih! Das stinkt!"*
pony and trap	crap *Scheiße*	"This game's a bit pony." *"Das Spiel ist ziemlich scheiße."*
pork pies (porkie pies)	lies *Lügen*	"He's always telling porkies." *"Der erzählt nichts als Lügen."*

J. Arthur Rank	wank *wichsen*	"He's having a J. Arthur." *'"Er holt sich einen runter."*
ginger beer	queer *schwul*	"He's a ginger beer." *"Das ist 'ne Schwuchtel."*
Queen Mum	bum *Hintern*	"Get off your Queen Mum." *"Krieg' mal deinen Hintern hoch."*
raspberry tart	fart *furzen*	"Who's dropped a raspberry?" *"Wer hat hier gefurzt?"*
Richard the Third	turd *Stück Scheiße*	"That bloke's a Richard!" *"Der Typ ist ein Scheißkerl!"*

Appendix 4 – Australian swearwords and insults
Anhang 4 – Australische Schimpfwörter und Beleidigungen

a **bludger**
Lazy person, layabout.
Faulenzer

bodgy
Of inferior quality.
Schrottig

"As cunning as a dunny rat!"
Very clever.
"Gerissen wie eine Kloratte", listig, raffiniert

a **drongo**
A dope, stupid person.
Trottel

figjam
People who have a high opinion of themselves.
Steht für "Fuck, I'm Good, Just Ask Me" und beschreibt eine eingebildete Person

a **fruit loop**
A fool.
Irrer

a galah
A fool or silly person.
Schwachkopf, Idiot

a mongrel
A despicable person.
Bastard

a ratbag
A mild insult.
Unruhestifter (freundschaftlich)

(to) root
Colloquial term for "to fuck".
Ficken

a root rat
Somebody who is constantly looking for sex.
Lustmolch, Schwerenöter

a sheep shagger
A New Zealander.
Schafficker, hier: Neuseeländer

shonky
Dubious, underhanded.
Zwielichtig, hinterhältig

"Show us ya jugs!"
"Show us your breasts!"
"Zeig' uns deine Titten!"

a slit-eyed fuck
A Chinaman.
Schlitzauge, Chinese

a whacker
An idiot, somebody who talks drivel.
Dummschwätzer; jemand, der nur Müll erzählt

"Who opened their lunch?"
"Who farted?"
"Wer hat gefurzt?"

Appendix 5 – Blasphemy
Anhang 5 – Blasphemische Schimpfwörter

Blasphemy is the taking of the Lord God's name in vain. Warning: Using any of the following blasphemous expressions/swearwords is almost certain to cause offense to any religious-minded people.

Blasphemie bedeutet Gotteslästerung. ***Vorsicht:*** *Die Verwendung der folgenden Schimpfwörter kann religiöse Gefühle verletzen. Daher gilt: Aufpassen, wo und bei wem man diese Ausdrücke verwendet!*

Blasphemous statements of frustration or exasperation:

Blasphemische Begriffe, die Frustration und Verärgerung ausdrücken:

"Jesus Christ!"
"Christ almighty!"
"Holy Christ!"
"Good God!"
"Oh my God!"
"For God's sake!"
"For Christ's sake!"
"God damn it!"
"Hell fire!"
"Oh hell!"
"Hell's bells!"
"For the love of God!"
"Christ above!"
"Holy shit!"
"Holy crap!"
"Jesus wept!"
"Sweet Jesus!"
"Jesus, Mary and Joseph!"
"Christ on a bike!"
"Jesus H. Christ!"

Appendix 6 – Intensifiers

Anhang 6 – Verstärkungswörter

"Bloody" (mild), "bleeding" (medium) and "fucking" (hard) are the three most popular intensifiers you can use with other insults. (For example: "Bloody sod!") Words that end with -ing are often spelt and pronounced without the g at the end: bleedin', friggin', etc.

Die folgenden drei Wörter lassen sich hervorragend mit anderen Kraftausdrücken kombinieren: "Bloody" (harmlos), "bleeding" (mittel) und "fucking" (heftig). Endet das Wort auf -ing, wird das g meistens nicht mitgesprochen und -geschrieben.